W9-AES-542

BASIC BIOGRAPHIES

Barack Obama

by Susan Kesselring

Barack Obama is the forty-fourth **president** of the United States. He is the first black person to have that job.

Barack Obama became the president of the United States in 2009.

Barack was born in Hawaii on August 4, 1961. His mom was a white woman from Kansas. His dad was a black man from Kenya, Africa. They met at **college**.

Barack grew up in Hawaii.

Barack lived with his mom and grandparents when he was young. He did not see his dad very much.

Barack's grandparents helped raise him.

Barack worked very hard in school. He went to college in California and New York. He went to school to become a **lawyer**. After law school Barack moved to Chicago, Illinois.

This is Barack when he was learning to be a lawyer.

Barack met Michelle at work. They fell in love. They got married and had two daughters, Malia and Sasha.

Barack and Michelle have two daughters, Malia (left) and Sasha (right).

Barack helped make laws for the United States. He wanted to make things better for all people.

Barack was a lawmaker in Washington DC.

Then, Barack wanted to be president. He told people about his ideas. Many people liked what he said.

Barack talked to crowds all around the country.

In November 2008, the people of the United States voted. They made Barack their president. He became president on January 20, 2009.

This is Barack on election night, November 4, 2008.

Now he lives in the **White House** with his family. They have a dog named Bo.

Barack likes to play with the family's dog.

Barack is very busy working for our country. But he still likes to be at home with Michelle, Malia, Sasha, and Bo.

The Obamas spend family time together in the White House.

Glossary

college (KOL-ij): College is a school people go to after high school. Barack went to college.

lawyer (LOY-ur): A lawyer is someone who helps others understand laws. Barack worked as a lawyer.

president (PREZ-uh-dent): The president is the leader of the United States. Barack became the president.

White House (WITE HOWSS): The White House is where the president lives and works. The White House is in Washington DC.

To Find Out More

Books

Edwards, Roberta. *Barack Obama: An American Story*. New York: Grosset and Dunlap, 2007.

Grimes, Nikki. *Barack Obama: Son of Promise, Child of Hope*. New York: Simon & Schuster, 2008.

Miller, Zenin. *It's Me, Zenin! President Barack Obama's Kid Neighbor*. Scotts Valley, CA: CreateSpace, 2009.

Winter, Jonah. *Barack*. New York: HarperCollins, 2009.

Web Sites

Visit our Web site for links about Barack Obama: *childsworld.com/links*

Note to Parents, Teachers, and Librarians: We routinely verify our Web links to make sure they are safe and active sites. So encourage your readers to check them out!

Index

Bo, 18, 20
born, 4
college, 4, 8
dad, 4, 6
grandparents, 6
laws, 12
lawyer, 8
mom, 4, 6
Obama, Malia, 10, 20
Obama, Michelle, 10, 20
Obama, Sasha, 10, 20
president, 2, 14, 16
White House, 18

About the Author

Susan Kesselring has taught all ages of children from preschool through grade 8. She has been a certified Reading Recovery teacher and director of a preschool. She loves to help children get excited about learning. Family, friends, books, music, and her dog, Lois Lane, are some of her favorite things.

On the cover: Barack Obama greeted the crowd in Chicago on election night, November 4, 2008.

Published by The Child's World®
1980 Lookout Drive • Mankato, MN 56003-1705
800-599-READ • www.childsworld.com

ACKNOWLEDGMENTS
The Child's World®: Mary Berendes, Publishing Director
The Design Lab: Design and production
Red Line Editorial: Editorial direction

PHOTO CREDITS: Morry Gash/AP Images, cover, 14, 22; Sándor F. Szabó/iStockphoto, cover; Chris Carlson/AP Images, 3; AP Images, 5, 7, 9; M. Spencer Green/AP Images, 11; Manuel Balc Ceneta/AP Images, 13; J. Pat Carter/AP Images, 15; Pablo Martinez Monsivais/AP Images, 17; Ron Edmonds/AP Images, 19; Alex Brandon/AP Images, 21

Printed in the United States of America in Mankato, Minnesota.
November 2009
F11460

LIBRARY OF CONGRESS CATALOGING-IN-PUBLICATION DATA
Kesselring, Susan.
 Barack Obama / by Susan Kesselring.
   p. cm. — (Basic biographies)
 Includes index.
 ISBN 978-1-60253-339-4 (library bound : alk. paper)
 1. Obama, Barack—Juvenile literature. 2. Presidents—United States—Biography—Juvenile literature. I. Title. II. Series.
 E908.K47 2010
 973.932092—dc22 [B]   2009029365

6/11